FLAMINGO
A PHOTOGRAPHER'S ODYSSEY

BY HARA

HARRY N. ABRAMS, INC., PUBLISHERS, NEW YORK

DEDICATION

For my mother, Anabel

And Ron, who believed in me

For Ernie, who supported me at crucial moments

And especially for Bill, who introduced me to Africa—and an experience that changed my life

Project Editor: Robert Morton
Text Editor: Cork Millner
Designer: Tom Lewis

Library of Congress Cataloging-in-Publication Data
Hara.
Flamingo: a photographer's odyssey / by Hara.
p. cm.
Includes bibliographical references (p. 128)
ISBN 0–8109–2511–7
1. Flamingos–Africa, East–Pictorial works. 2. Photography of
birds–Africa, East. 3. Hara–Journeys–Africa, East. 4. Africa,
East–Description and travel,–1981 5. Photographers–United
States–Biography. I. Title.
QL696.C56H37 1991
508.676—dc20   91-8757

CONTENTS

From the distance,

an amazing sight appeared

As we approached,

the vision became clearer

I could not believe what I saw

— a mirage, an island all in pink

A million flamingos

softly coloring the desert harshness

Never had I seen

anything more beautiful

THE PINK ISLAND

THE PINK

Flamingos!"

I leaned forward in my seat, not sure that I had heard him over the sound of the Cessna's engine.

"What?"

"Flamingos!" Herman Steyn, the bush pilot, repeated louder, twisting halfway around to see my expression.

There was a pink haze on the lake just ahead. Flamingos? In the middle of the great Rift Valley? With the exception of several soda-crusted lakes, the valley—a jagged scar stretching a thousand miles across the eastern face of Africa—is a desert of dead volcanos, ragged cliffs and staggering 120 degree heat. How could a bird as delicate as a flamingo survive here?

Herman nudged the controls and we dipped closer. Now the shimmering pink vision filled my view as if a million rose petals had been spread by an unseen hand onto the glass-smooth water of Lake Natron.

"Can we get any closer?" I asked.

They appeared to be floating...

Herman smiled and eased the tiny plane, a lonely speck of metal in the vast arena of African sky, into a descending turn. The spiral tightened as we flew below the level of the volcanic craters and now the pink bodies became a blur, melting into the reflections of the lake's mirrored surface. The scene was surreal; a shimmering mirage inspired by the heat reflecting off the lake. Then it came into focus, crystallizing into an incredible mass of living birds.

As we completed the first circle, I leaned closer to Herman. "This is the most fantastic thing I have ever seen! Can we fly over them one more time?"

ISLAND

He twisted the plane into a tight turn, banking so steeply that I was able to look straight down at the colony. I braced my camera against my body to steady it from the engine's vibration, and compressed my vision into the viewfinder. With no relationship to sky or water, I saw a great pink cloud floating in a fathomless blue sky. The camera's motor drive clicked against my cheek as I captured image after image.

"More over there," Herman said, nodding toward the other side of the lake, about eight miles away. Pushing the throttle forward, he headed for a pink mist in the distance. As we approached, low on the water, a dozen flamingos spread their scarlet-streaked, black-edged wings, ran across the water, and flapping their wings in wide arcs, took to the air. I felt guilty about terrifying them in this way, but their beauty was irresistible. Long and slender, like arrows, the great birds glided just above the surface, their wings caressing the wind.

We circled again, and through the camera's viewfinder, the intermingling of sky, water, and pink gave me the illusion of drifting effortlessly in space. Flamingos glided into view, then slipped out of the frame, leaving only the blue vista.

Then, the drone of the engine became strangely silent, and the only sound I heard was my heartbeat, and the brushing of feathers against the air. I felt as if I were plunging into a great azure pool, arching into its depths: bubbles surrounded me, coming from above, from below, streaming across my face. I was immersed, weightless in a wondrous water ballet of crimson and

An island of pink —

white and blue. Then, as if coming up from a dive, I angled toward the surface, then hesitated, not wanting to leave this sensation.

The plane lurched sideways, jerking me back to reality. A great cracking sound followed and a white spray geysered around us. We had crashed into something. I was thrown violently forward. *"Oh, God,"* I thought, *"we've hit the water."* Herman wrenched the plane free from the lake and pulled it into a climb. There was a second of eerie silence. Then Herman turned in his seat, hands white, gripping the controls. "We should both be dead," he said.

I swallowed, my mouth dry, and nodded. *"Yes, I know,"* I thought, letting the fear ebb. *"I know. But those flamingos…Did you see those flamingos!"*

Back at the airfield in Nairobi, Herman and I stood looking at the plane. The wheels and belly of the fuselage were caked with a white powder. We had hit the alkaline water with a wheel, spraying the underside with a layer of soda. Herman, his face still pale with fear, broke the silence: "Our little dip in the lake was like hitting concrete at 150 miles per hour. We really should have flipped over and disintegrated." He cleared his throat and went on, explaining how the horizon had become lost in the reflection of the water—a common cause of air crashes in Africa. But his voice began to fade from my consciousness, replaced by images of flamingos soaring, scarlet and white, graceful against the blue of the lake.

I knew at that moment I must capture the beauty of these great birds, learn how they survived in the cauldron of the Rift Valley—to *share* their experience.

Looking once more at the soda-crusted plane, I knew that this time I had been very lucky. What I didn't know was that my affair with the flamingos would be a far more terrifying adventure than I could ever have imagined.

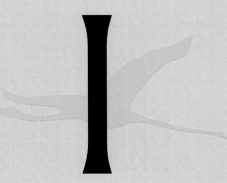

I

A PROPER SAFARI

A Proper

The microphone clicked and the flight attendant's voice came over the intercom: "Ladies and gentlemen, we have arrived in Nairobi, the capital of the African republic of Kenya. Please keep your seat belts on until…"

I relaxed in my seat. I had made it. Over the last year-and-a-half "Project Flamingo"—as I had dubbed it—had constantly been on my mind.

I could find very little written about flamingos and learned less from anyone who had photographed them. I discovered there were two kinds in Africa, the Greater Flamingo and the Lesser Flamingo.

There are six kinds found throughout the world, each with their own markings, size, eating, and breeding habits. In Africa, the Greater and Lesser Flamingos are the only two species that live side by side because they do not compete for food, though both feed in the water. The brightly plumed five-foot tall Greater Flamingo (scientific name *Phoenicopterus ruber roseus*, meaning "crimson winged" in Latin) dips near the bottom when feeding. The Lesser Flamingo skims the surface. The Lesser has its own genus, *Phoenicopterus minor*, (formerly Phoeniconaias). Its specific name *minor* seems to fit when one realizes that this bird is two feet shorter than its cousin. The Lesser is the most numerous and the only true African flamingo as the Greater Flamingo migrates to the lakes in the Rift Valley from the north. Yet, even with the differences in number and size, these elegant creatures live in close harmony on the shallow soda-crusted lakes of East Africa. There, in this inhospitable environment, the African flamingo has remained a bird of mystery. I was resolved to explore these mysteries.

The flamingo, with its delicate pink and flaming red plumage, has always been an object of fascination and beauty. The first known representation of the flamingo was scratched by a Stone Age artist on a cave wall in southern

SAFARI

Spain around 5000 BC. The Egyptians revered the flamingo as the living embodiment of the sun-god Ra and used drawings of the great bird as the hieroglyphic symbol for the color crimson.

During the Middle Ages, the flamingo was largely forgotten. But during the age of discovery, the birds were encountered in Africa and Asia, and then in the newly explored Americas.

It was my ambition to photograph the flamingo's crimson beauty and regal elegance on the blue waters of the eastern African lakes. And thereupon set out to arrange a safari. Realizing how difficult it would be to get close to the flamingo breeding colonies, I thought that perhaps a shallow-draft boat would be the answer. I found a company in the U.S. which manufactured a collapsible canoe that could hold two people plus photography equipment. The fragile boat was shipped to Kenya. Perfect, I thought. As far as I could tell, no one had attempted to approach the African flamingos by boat. Why, I wondered? It seemed so easy.

For provisions and supplies in Africa, I relied on Herman Steyn, the bush pilot, with whom I had had the close brush with death. Herman agreed to lease to me a complete set of safari equipment, including a Toyota Landcruiser. He would also hire out two of his employees and a cook. Each had years of safari experience and was an old hand in the bush. These arrangements were supplemented by two butane-powered refrigerators, one for storing the 300 rolls of film I was taking, and the other to preserve food and provide the luxury of a cold drink in the Rift Valley's intense heat. It was beginning to look like what the British called a "proper safari."

I had sent a telex informing Herman of my arrival, but, walking into the Nairobi terminal, I searched in vain for his friendly face. He was nowhere in sight. I called his office and was told that he had "disappeared, to avoid certain problems."

"And the safari equipment?" I asked.

"Sorry, all his assets are tied up by the

government," came the answer.

I hung up the telephone—numb. I should have known. Herman was always, in his words, "arm wrestling" with the authorities over some venture or other. He had gone from being a "great white hunter" prior to the ban on hunting in Kenya, to becoming an aggressive businessman. Now his ventures had caught up with him. And me. I had no equipment, no guides. The proper safari was in shambles.

So here I was in the middle of the Nairobi airport with seven metal Halliburton camera cases, a suitcase, and no place to go. Exhausted after the halfway-round-the-world flight from California, I decided that the first thing to do was get some sleep. Dragging my camera cases to a shady area outside the terminal, I lined them up end to end—a security system I had invented while traveling alone—stretched out on top and fell asleep.

I woke up after a couple hours feeling refreshed and called an American couple, Roberta and Bill Fonville, whom I had met on an earlier photo assignment. The Fonvilles owned a house outside Nairobi.

"Ah yes, that sounds like Herman," Bill Fonville chuckled when I told him of my pre-dicament. "I'll send someone from our place to pick you up. Perhaps we can help you out; there's some safari equipment we've had stored in a shed for ages."

The Fonvilles' equipment, which hadn't been used for many years, was in terrible shape. The old green tent I unfolded had faded and the canvas was rotting, as were several canvas tarpaulins I unearthed. Since no tents were being manufactured in or imported into Nairobi, I had to keep these fragile rags for my safari. I then selected a couple of folding camp chairs, some scratchy wool blankets, two cooking pots, a rusty machete, a knife, a shovel, and a collapsible toilet and shower tent. To this dusty pile was added a handmade wooden toilet seat. The varnish was peeling and I figured that my worst worry would be getting splinters. I had to smile at this charming contraption. When I picked it up, the spindly wooden legs that were supposed to support the seat dangled from strings like wind chimes.

The Fonvilles told me that I could hire a couple of workers from a local farm to join me on safari. "Probably never been in the bush before, but they'll do," Bill said. "Only one problem—they're Kikuyus, tribal Africans, don't speak English." He smiled broadly. "Not to worry, we'll make up a little list of Swahili words for you."

Roberta Fonville looked at me with concern. "You sure you want to go out there by yourself? A girl alone in Maasailand? It's hard for the Maasai to live in such a terrible place."

"We'll see. I may not be as delicate as I look." I smiled. "But then, neither are the flamingos."

She nodded, then said, " 'Hara.' It's such an unusual name."

"Everyone wants to know about that," I said. "My father was in the military stationed in Japan when I was a child and my Japanese nanny gave me the name, 'Hara.' It means 'soul.' "

Roberta gave me a friendly pat on the arm. "Lovely, a lovely name. Since I saw you here on your last safari, I've seen some of your work in *National Geographic*. I know you'll be able to get what you want with the flamingos." She looked at the pile of dusty canvas, tables and chairs and sighed. "I hope our shabby store of equipment will be of some help."

"Yes, thank you so much." I started to feel better. All I needed was food supplies and a four-wheel-drive vehicle. When the Nairobi rental agency told me that a Land Rover would cost $100 a day, I groaned. I figured it would take

Dusty canvas, two Kikuyu tribesmen, and a beat-up Land Rover . . .

three weeks, perhaps a month to photograph the flamingos. More than two thousand dollars to rent a Land Rover cut severely into my $4,000 cash reserve.

The next shock came when I went to pick up the canoe that I had shipped in. At the customs office the young clerk adjusted his steel-rimmed glasses and intoned, "The duty on all sporting goods is 150 percent of declared value." He told me the amount in Kenyan shillings and it came to one thousand dollars. I was livid. But my entreaties might have well been spoken to a wall. I had to have the canoe, so I posted a bond for the amount of duty.

Back at the Fonvilles I set up the collapsible rubber canoe, sighing with relief that it worked. Perfect. I could visualize myself paddling stealthily under the cover of a rosy dawn to the flamingo breeding grounds, a serene, romantic trip on a crystal blue lake. I had forgotten for the moment what I had read about the savage heat, the foul-smelling soda lakes and the dangerous mud flats.

Now I had to assemble my staff. The message that I needed a couple of local tribesmen to assist me on the safari had been spread by the African grapevine: the Fonvilles told someone in Nairobi, who relayed it to someone on a bus, who told it to a native walking the road, who passed it around the villages. Three days later, the names of two Kikuyu tribesmen, Wammasai and Wambugo, came back via the same grapevine. I had no idea what either of them looked like, or what experience they had, but I had the name of their village.

After the Land Rover was packed with safari equipment, I drove out of Nairobi to pick up the men. Nairobi, the capitol of Kenya, was always a pleasant surprise for me. Named after the Maasai word, N'erobi, which means "place of cold water," the city was built at the beginning of the century as a rail depot. Although it is located only a few degrees from the equator, its climate, due to the elevation above sea level, is dry and comfortable, a pleasant 75 to 85 degrees most of the year. Tall, modern buildings vie with English colonial architecture for space. At the old-fashioned Norfolk Hotel one expects to see parasols and flowing Victorian gowns, reminders of the city's English settler heritage. Evenings can be spent sipping Pimm's #1 Cup under the gigantic thorn tree at the New Stanley Hotel.

Nairobi is a well-planned capitol with wide streets and arcades. It is hard to believe that

The roar of my engine awakens a sleeping lion

as late as 1907 it was little more than a tent city where warriors from the bush still speared Europeans. In 1961 the first six people buried in Nairobi cemetery had been killed by lions. I remember reading a Kenya newspaper on the airplane which headlined a basketball victory by the hometown team, then carried a two-inch story at the bottom of the second page which said: LION KILLS MAN IN LOCAL VILLAGE.

Outside Nairobi, I drove past verdant fields of vegetables until arriving at the last hillside farm village, an enclave of shabby wooden buildings, roofed with corrugated metal. A tall, lean-boned tribesman in his mid-thirties trotted from behind a house. He wore an orange nylon pullover shirt and a black leather cap.

A cheetah watches over the hunting grounds

Hippos live in harmony with all the lake's creatures

Giraffes gallop beside the Road

"Wambugo." He carefully pronounced his name and smiled.

"*Jambo*." Hello, I answered, using one of my few words of Swahili.

Another man, very dark, short and muscular with a wide nose and black eyes, stepped toward me. He shook my hand in an exaggerated up-and-down motion and pointed to himself, "Wammasai!"

Both of them carried bright cotton kikoys in which they had tightly wrapped their few belongings. Natives use the kikoy to carry everything from food to babies. When not in use it can be tied around the body as a garment. I wondered uneasily whether Wammasai and Wambugo carried enough to last weeks, perhaps a month in the bush.

They both stood in the dust staring at me, no doubt wondering what they were supposed to do for this pale-skinned woman, wearing a blouse and khaki shorts, tall as a Maasai, with waist-length blond hair. Neither knew they were going on safari to photograph flamingos, nor did they know how long they'd be gone—a week, a year? They didn't even know how much they were being paid. And I had no way of telling them.

Both were Kikuyus of Kenya. In the late 19th century this tribe of hunters and farmers had been encouraged to emulate the Englishman's values and religion. They were rewarded by servitude. Caught between two worlds, the Kikuyus were not anxious to find a world of their own. Initiatives and plans for work were unfamiliar to them. Wammasai and Wambugo, for example, two farmers, were apparently willing to trek anywhere, with no guarantee.

On the outskirts of Nairobi I stopped at a small general store to shop for food. We loaded up on cases of Coca Cola and Tusker Beer, added tins of canned meat, several boxes of vegetables, then, almost as an afterthought, a forty-pound bag of potatoes. Wammasai and Wambugo gestured to show me what they wanted, a sack of

corn grain, which, when mixed with water, made the African food staple known as *posho*.

In the store, my eye was caught by a little plastic tray with a picture of a giraffe and the words "Kenya" in red sweeping letters. *A proper coffee serving tray for an improper safari*, I thought, tossing it in with the rest of the purchases. I counted out $200 worth of shillings from my dwindling cash supply, had Wammasai and Wambugo add it on the top of the bulging Land Rover—and we were off to one of harshest, most unforgiving regions of the Rift Valley.

I was on my way. Feeling good.

Sure, it was a bare-bones safari: old rotting camping gear, two African farmers who had never been in the bush before, and a crumpled list of Swahili words. I was also aware that Wammasai and Wambugo were totally dependent on me for survival. Before our safari ended they would name me, "*Mama Ngumu*"—Tough Mama.

...off to find adventure

2

Dreams and Dilemmas

DREAMS AND

I drove south past fenced, dusty grassland and leafless bushes that gave the country a monotonous gray appearance. The paved road suddenly disintegrated into dirt and the fences ended. The bush became denser and the flat-topped acacia trees, festooned with hanging ornaments—the round nests of weaver birds—were common. Termite hills up to three feet high looked like towering sand castles built by some enterprising children. We passed rusty abandoned vehicles and a few Africans walking alongside the road. Children waved and shouted "Jambo." My companions and I waved, but remained silent, watching the ever changing landscape.

I got a glimpse of several groups of scrawny humpbacked cattle attended by the Maasai, who were once the fiercest tribe in Africa. Black and angular as the burnt skeleton of a tree, the Maasai clothe themselves in one-piece ochre colored robes called *shukas*. A nomadic people who tend herds of cattle and goats, they nourish themselves on a diet of cow's blood and milk which they carry sloshing in gourds at their sides.

Seeing these Maasai reminded me of a story I had heard. Maasai folklore tells of a young warrior who, while kneeling at a pool to drink, saw in the water's reflection a red bird with plumage more brilliant than he had ever seen. Wanting to hold such magnificence in his hand, he sprang up, but there was no sign of the bird in the empty sky. The Maasai wandered from place to place searching for this exotic creature and his quest continued until he became very old. Then one day he heard of a vast lake in the distance where red birds beyond counting might be found.

He began an arduous journey across the range of mountains that overlooked the lake. With the last of his strength he reached the summit and lay down to rest. He gazed into the distance searching for the elusive red bird, but he could see nothing. Wondering if his life had been spent in vain, he closed his eyes, then saw

DILEMMAS

on the back of his eyelids the vision of the bird he had seen in his youth.

As his dying soul left the shell of his body, a feather of bright, burning red drifted down from the sky and came to rest in his open hand.

I hoped my pursuit of the flamingo would be more tangible than the Maasai's.

We continued across the Ngong Hills, the dust rising in a white plume behind us as the Land Rover groaned on through the thickening 100 degree heat. The land became bare and bony with only a few whiskers of grass. Swirling dust devils, like genies from a bewitched bottle, curled hundreds of feet into the air and rushed off with the wind.

My intention was to drive south to Lake Natron where I had seen the pink island from the air, find a campsite beside the lake, set up my bird blinds, and begin photographing. But first I would try to circle the smaller Lake Magadi where the map showed a dotted trail looping around its shore.

Alkaline lakes shine like teardrops on the face of Africa

We were now in Maasailand which slashes like a scimitar from Lake Victoria on the eastern edge of Kenya across Lake Natron and into Tanzania. I planned to set up my campsite near the center of Maasailand, on the cutting edge of the blade. We would be on the floor of the Rift Valley.

And suddenly there it was before us, the greatest gorge on the African continent, indeed, the greatest on any land surface in the world. The Rift Valley was eerie and tremendous, up to 200 miles wide and several thousand feet deep, studded with craters, like a moonscape; an enormous tract of harsh land almost devoid of shade or color green, a land that becomes increasingly hostile as it opens into the chain of shallow alkaline lakes and soda flats. On these caustic flats, I had been told, the temperature can rise to 140 degrees.

It is here that African flamingos live. And thrive. Here the flamingo needs no defense. The soda lakes discourage all but the hardiest predatory animals and birds. It was this unforgiving and consuming environment that drew me forward like a magnet.

For a moment we teetered on the edge of this alien world looking at the shadowy cliffs of the Nguruman escarpment in the distance. Then, putting the truck into gear, we headed into the valley.

The Land Rover careened over rocks the size of footballs, rattling us around inside the cab like dried peas in a gourd. At times the steering wheel jerked from my hands. Branches of stunted acacia trees scraped against the side of the truck, reminding me of chalk scratching on a blackboard. I was concentrating so hard on driving, missing the larger rocks, trees and bushes, that I couldn't see more than a few feet ahead, nor could I glance at Wambugo's or Wammasai's faces. But I knew they were wide-eyed, holding on for dear life, thinking, *"What is this crazy woman doing to us? She's surely carrying us to our death!"*

Then the steering wheel flew out of my hands and we dropped into a ditch. SNAP! The Land Rover jerked sideways, came to a jolting stop and all the provisions on the roof tumbled over the hood and exploded onto the powdery dirt.

I clambered out into the choking dust. One of my fears was that the battered Land Rover would break down beyond repair. Good thing they built them like tanks, I thought, patting the burning hood like it was a faithful friend. It wasn't stuck in the ditch. I could grind my way out.

I motioned for Wammasai and Wambugo to load the gear back on the roof, then, as I bent over to pick up a box, *I saw it:* a wondrous pink haze seeming to float in the far distance on the surface of the lake.

Flamingos.

I grabbed my camera with the 300mm lens and looked through the viewfinder. The cliffs on the opposite side of the valley were shadowed, but before them, reflected in the mirror of the lake, was a gossamer crimson cloud. I had found them. All I had to do now was find a way to get close enough to photograph them.

Roping the provisions back on the roof, we pushed ahead on the trackless plateau, past grass that now grew so tall it brushed against the windshield, blocking the view. I thought that any minute we would break out onto the trail that led around the lake, certain that beyond the next bush, over the next ridge, we would be presented with a breathtaking vista of blue horizon, broken by a line of millions of flamingos. After a few miles I knew the worst had happened. We had been circling in hopeless loops. We were lost in a maze of bushes and grass. And, now, ahead, was a deep gully that blocked our path.

I got out and started to walk alone through the high brush in what seemed to be the right direction to the escarpment overlooking the lake. After hiking a quarter of a mile into the unknown, the thorns of bony acacia trees snagging my hair, I began to feel the first tinge of fear.

Darkness, one of the elements I feared the most, would soon be on us. Quickly retracing my steps, I found Wammasai and Wambugo crouched under the sparse shade of an acacia

The trail of death was obvious

tree. They were scared. Why had they been brought to this place? Their lives had been spent in a lush green farming community and now they were here, in this wasteland.

What should I do? Camp where we were? No, even a slight breeze would erase our tire tracks. We had to go back. Turning the truck around, I followed our trail until we reached a widening path that I hadn't noticed before. This led to a rocky causeway that crossed to the other side of the shallow lake; to the flamingos. I later learned that it had been built by the British some forty years previously.

Something caught my eye at the water's edge. There in the mud lay a dead pelican, its bright plumage now a dull gray, its wings splayed

outward in a hopeless gesture of dying. Shaking off this presence of death, I drove across the causeway and on the other side climbed up a steep bank to the top of the escarpment. From this vantage point high on the cliff, I peered over the steep drop—then my heart sank. What had seemed from so far away to be flamingos was only a crusty area of pink soda. Staggered by the heat and jolted almost senseless by the drive, I felt my resolve ebbing away. No! There were flamingos on this lake and I would find them.

Driving across the causeway, I had seen another chalky bridge that led to the northwest corner of the lake and I drove back on my original path until I was on its surface. The sun was lowering to the edge of the cliff when I saw a familiar pink haze mirrored on the lake. Another illusion? I drove on, thinking this must be it. This *had* to be it. Then, strangely, the line of the pink began to take on a life of its own. *It moved!* Tiny fluttering movements, specks of black, layers of white—flamingos. Thousands of them, hundreds of thousands of pink and white flamingos.

Elated, I pulled off the causeway and drove up an incline until I found a high place that overlooked the lake and blocked us from the birds' view. I switched off the motor.

Silence.

For several minutes I stared at the rose-hued gathering of birds. Yes, this was the place where we would make camp. As a campsite, it left much to be desired—a place in the middle of the Rift Valley across from the Nguruman escarpment and completely exposed to the merciless African sun. The terrain was a rubbled expanse of lava rock, the soil parched and scorched to ashen powder. A solitary dead tree, the black skeletal remains of an acacia which had long ago given up its struggle to survive, marked the center of the site.

But in this hostile environment we will be safe, I thought, for the heat provided security. Here under the sun, where there was no fresh water, even the hardiest predators would not linger. I had accepted misery for a relative degree of safety.

Less than a quarter mile away, down a gradual slope was Lake Magadi, its alkaline surface encrusted by soda that varied in color from stark white to bright pink. The caustic vapors rising from the bitter waters could bring the surface temperature at midday to a point unbearable

A waterbuck shares the shore

(OVERLEAF) White pelicans prepare for flight

The droughts' receding waterline claims the life
of a Thompson's gazelle

to human life. Yet, this devastating environment was the home of hundreds of thousands of the most exquisite and seemingly fragile creatures.

"*Mzuri sana.*" Good, I said. Very good.

Wammasai and Wambugo nodded and the three of us nearly fell out of the Land Rover with exhaustion, muscles tense from bracing our bodies against the jolting ride.

I pointed to the camp gear on the roof then to the spindly tree. "*Chukua.*" Carry.

Wammasai and Wambugo unloaded the truck then helped me set up my tent, tying one end to the acacia tree. Wammasai whacked apart a dead bush with the machete and made a campfire. Then the two of them bundled up a tarp, their sack of *posho,* and cautiously walked 100 yards up a slight hill where they attached a canvas tarp to a small acacia and built another campfire. Too tired to cook a meal, we ate from the tins of meat and drank warm Tusker beer. As we ate in exhausted silence, the evening shadows lengthened, heralding the darkness to follow. The air became heavy, the life gone out it.

Nightfall. The one thing that I knew could weaken my resolve. I remembered the words of Beryl Markham: "It is the host of all my darkest fears." Yes, I thought, there is no darkness like a moonless night in the African bush. Slowly the night enveloped me and my tiny camp, a tiny pinpoint of life in the vast arena of the valley.

Then, from somewhere in the fading light, I heard the deep growl of a lion. I froze. Wammasai and Wambugo hunched next to their tent, their eyes wide, reflecting the dancing light of their campfire. They looked at me as if I could make the sound go away.

The lion roared again.

Crawling into my tent, I stretched out on the two dusty blankets that were folded over the rocks, and pulled a kikoy topsheet over me. I felt foolish, like a child hiding from goblins and witches. Having come half-way around the world to pursue this dream I *had* to confront my fear. If this is what each night was going to be like I might as well get used to it.

I closed my eyes. In the blackness, I saw a lion snarling by my side, and at the foot of my open-ended tent a hooded cobra poised ready to strike.

I struggled for a frozen moment like a gazelle caught in the grips of a lion, then surrendered to sleep, my escape from the fear.

There is no darkness like a moonless night in the African bush

(OVERLEAF) *Lake Magadi — a barren prospect*

My camp was a lonely speck in the great Rift Valley

3

Lure of a Legend

LURE OF

Amber blades of light sliced at the darkness. And at the end of my bed, silhouetted by the coming dawn, was the raised head of a cobra. I started to cry out. Then felt foolish as I recognized my tennis shoe wiggling on my foot. At my side, the lion now materialized into the shadow of the Land Rover on my canvas tent.

A view of Lake Magadi filled the triangular end of the tent and on the horizon rose a great wall of billowing clouds through which the sun light broke and streamed across the sky in a golden fan. I breathed in deeply. The smell of dew and dust filled the air.

Wammasai and Wambugo came down the slope relieved to have survived the night. They looked questioningly at me. *What now?* I greeted them with an enthusiastic *"Jambo!"* and began to set up our camp with the idea of making it as close to a proper safari as our shabby equipment would allow. One folding table was designated as the kitchen and was placed in the spider-web shadow of the acacia tree. Dragging two folding chairs and another table under the overhanging flap of the tent, I called this area the "veranda." Several three-liter plastic jugs comprised our water supply, and I set them in the shade of the tent. A rope strung from my tent to the tree became the clothesline.

Next, I devised a daily work schedule. The discipline of an ordered routine would be essential even for our tiny safari. This I had learned in Kenya while watching the British,

Sunrise

A Legend

Base camp— home for a month

whose punctilious observance of afternoon tea under the most harrowing of conditions made survival in the bush a civilized affair.

The working day began at 4:30 AM when I was awakened by Wambugo's whispered, "Okay, *Memsahib*," and heard the tray with the strong coffee being slid toward me under the tent flap. I had had to show him how to boil water, then drop in a handful of grounds and pour off the brew into a cup. Those first minutes of waking, breathing the aroma of Kenyan coffee, were the most luxurious of the day.

His wake-up call complete, Wambugo would trudge up the slope to his camp and rouse Wammasai who would then wait by my tent. In the predawn haze I could see his motionless silhouette.

"*Jambo*, Wammasai."

"*Mzuri sana* mama." Very good mama, he would reply in a respectful tone and heft the big tripod and attached camera onto his shoulder. We always started to the lake's edge before dawn to avoid detection by the flamingos. Slowly, our feet feeling the way, we picked our way around the lava rocks until we reached the bird blind I had established on the shore. After Wammasai helped me set up the camera, he would return to camp, leaving me alone in the darkness with the sleeping flamingo colony.

With Wammasai's help I had built two bird blinds, weaving thick marsh grass from the lake over stick frames. One in particular was very successful. I had noticed a little inlet with fresh

(OVERLEAF) I chose a site out of the flamingos' view

Weaving marsh grass to build bird blinds

spring water on the edge of the lake where the flamingos would come to drink in the mornings. The place I had chosen was also in the shadow of a six-foot cliff so the flamingos wouldn't see the outine of the blinds against the sky and think it was a predator. A perfect place to hide. We constructed two mats about the size of a double bed out of marsh grass. One of these served as the floor of the blind and the other the roof, which we propped up with sticks. We added a pile of rocks at the front and shrubbery for camouflage. Each morning before first light, I would crawl on my belly into this grassy hut and wait for sunrise. And snakes.

I was terrified of snakes. Before sneaking into the blind I would spear the darkness with a flashlight beam, expecting that the next thrust of light would reveal the cowl of a deadly cobra, or that dozens of serpents would emerge from the matted green and brown grass, slithering over one another. With these thoughts in mind, I would ease onto the mat each day tense with fear.

One morning I was propped up on my elbows in the blind, shooting a group of flamingos that had moved in close, when a rat sprang out of the grass, crawled under my chin and stopped. My first impulse was to scream. But the flamingos were closer than they had never been. I *had* to get them on film. I clicked away. Finally, the rat sniffed my skin, wrinkled his nose and walked away. I relaxed. At least it wasn't a snake.

The other blind was, I thought, a clever innovation: I used the four-sided canvas toilet tent. It had quickly become evident that the tent's intended function as a water closet—as the British would say—was ludicrous in this wild country. Besides, it was an oven in the heat. I set the wooden toilet seat up on its spindly legs—the open bush would do fine—and erected the tent as my blind.

The flamingos soon became accustomed to the green toilet tent in their midst and would feed or drink as close to it as 60 feet. When I popped my head over the top after finishing a morning photo session, they would scatter in a flurry of feathers and cacophony of squawks to a distance of about 300 feet. There they would feel safe.

Alone in the blind, as dawn spread its light over the lake, I would hear the first murmurs of the flamingo colony. It was a sound not unlike a symphony orchestra tuning up before a concert: first the string section and woodwinds

The Greater Flamingo stands taller

The Lesser Flamingo appears more delicate

as played by the Lesser Flamingos, followed by the honking calls of the Greater Flamingos, the orchestra's clarinets, trumpets, and French horns. This crescendo of peeping, chirping, squabbling and honking always made me smile.

There were many more Lesser Flamingos than Greater Flamingos in this colony I was photographing. The Greaters, true to their name, towered over the Lessers, long necks extending like periscopes bobbing in a whitecapped sea of feathers. Yet size made no difference as far as their ability to live in harmony.

Both stalked the shallow lake for food, their necks hooked toward the surface, beaks swishing back and forth in the warm algae-rich water. Strangely, the flamingo's head is suspended

(OVERLEAF) *Skimming the mirrored surface for a meal of blue-green algae*

in the water upside down, the curved crown entering first, the black beak pointed backwards.

As social etiquette and cuisine differ between cultures, so do the eating habits and diets of the Greater and Lesser flamingos. The Lessers dip their beaks into the water then walk forward a few steps, like plump matrons grazing at a buffet. Waving its head from side to side with a rapid "dabbing" motion, the Lesser Flamingo's beak penetrates the water little more than half an inch below the surface. The bill skims the blue-green algae (called *Spirulina*), trapping it in the lamellae, furry ridges of hair and tiny teeth that act as filters. The water spills out the other side of the beak. Although gallons of water pass through the beak during the feeding process, the flamingo does not drink this concentrated concoction of salt, soda, sulphate and fluoride.

After eating, the birds wade to drink and rinse at the fresh water springs that edge the lake. Many times the only available water gushes from hot geysers, which come to the surface at temperatures near the boiling point. The birds are able to drink it as we would a hot cup of coffee, but their legs can't take the scalding temperature and they jump from one foot to the other, "hot-footing" it away from the water. During

this agitated process, the birds dip the tips of their beaks just under the surface, then throw back their heads and swallow. This method traps very little liquid and is repeated over and over while they continue this strange dance.

Greater Flamingos feed deeper, submerging their heads close to the bottom. They stalk steadily forward, searching for their diet of brine-shrimp, insect larvae, small mollusks and crustaceans. If the nourishment is meager, they stand in place and paddle with their webbed feet to stir up the mud. This loosens the surface so that larger crustaceans and mollusks float free and can be sucked into the bill.

If the water becomes too deep for wading, both species of flamingos swim while feeding. They do so by dabbling in much the same way as ducks or swans, but appear terribly ungainly because of their short tails and the fact that their long, bent legs stick up out of the water behind them. In this manner they feed in water up to three feet deep.

No matter where the birds feed, they are a noisy, densely-packed group, like shoppers at a Macy's sale. The bargain basement feeding is interspersed with a constant bickering that drowns out all other sounds. While vying for

Flamingos dip their beaks to drink from hot pools

a choice eating space a bird may swing its head like a club, striking another bird on the side or rear. The bird that was hit simply moves a few steps and resumes feeding.

After the flamingos finish their morning meal they scatter, adopting a double-wing span distance from one another and spending most of the heat of the day preening, splashing water over their plumage and combing feathers with their beaks. By five o'clock when the temperature usually decreased by a few degrees, the flamingos start to come together again in feeding groups. This continues until dark when the birds scatter to deeper waters.

To do my photography, I worked rapidly in the morning light, many times focusing with a 600mm lens on one flamingo as it fed and interacted with the other birds. I had to work fast because the temperature—100 degrees at first light—quickly increased. By 8:00 AM it was 120 degrees and nearly impossible to continue working. My black-bodied Nikon camera became too hot to touch. I would wave for Wammasai and he would trot down the slope to carry my camera and tripod back to camp. Although he performed all his duties without question or any murmur of protest, I sometimes wondered if he

didn't think the *Memsahib* a little loony. After all, what was I doing hiding from a bunch of birds in a straw hut with my hands gripped around a thick black pipe that made whirring noises, a sound that he referred to as, "boom, taki-taki." I tried to explain with sign language, and one day it must have all registered in his mind that we were making a picture book. From then on he became intensely interested in the work and readily performed whatever tasks were required.

Wambugo never attempted to understand. He whistled continuously, blowing more air than sound, and snapped his fingers to a tune that only he heard. He earned the title of chief camp cook and laundryman. He scrubbed my clothes so vigorously in a plastic tub that they soon wore thin. Whatever he was doing, Wambugo felt the need for long pauses while he mopped his brow under his black leather cap.

Clothes were a problem. It was simply too hot to wear any. At first I wore shorts and a blouse and slipped leather thongs on my feet. I had brought along a bikini and tried that for several days. I had no fear of getting sunburned, even under the equatorial sun, because most of my time was spent in the shade. Standing in the mid-day sun for very long could cause

(OVERLEAF) *Counting the birds proves difficult*

Preening—the beak combs each feather

sunstroke—or be fatal. Eventually, I decided against wearing the bikini in the bush as African women never show the lower portions of their bodies. I finally wrapped a kikoy, which also served as a sheet and tablecloth, around my body. I would dip it in water and fold it around me during the midday heat, a pleasure that soon faded as the cloth whipped dry in the hot wind.

After the morning's session, Wambugo prepared breakfast, the cornmeal *posho* mixed with water for the two of them, and a burnt potato for me. The boxes of fresh vegetables had quickly spoiled and the canned meat I found impossible to eat. I gave the tins to Wammasai and Wambugo who considered meat a rare treat. Potatoes, coffee, Coca-Cola, and hot Tusker beer became my daily staples. At first I tried to maintain proper safari dining habits by eating the potato from a plate with a knife and fork. But each time I tried to stab or cut it, the charred object rolled around the plate like a billiard ball. I gave up and dug into its husk with my fingers, gnawing away like a lioness over a fresh kill.

My only visitor in this isolated campsite was a small brown mouse that I discovered while moving some boxes into the tent's shade. He scurried behind a box, darting over the burning lava rock, but I could still see him, twitching his tail in time to thin squeaks. Rats were one thing, a furry mouse another. This animal I could live with, and I smiled, feeling an immediate kinship. We would survive together in this punishing landscape. He adopted me as his tent mate.

In the heat of the day I would sit under the shaded veranda of my tent marking each canister of film that had been shot and then sealing it in a plastic bag to keep out the powdery African dust. Next I would record camera settings and various other technical data and jot some observations about the birds in my log book. If the heat hadn't become too stifling, I would read from Leslie Brown's book, *The Mystery of the Flamingos*, a small volume I had come across in a Nairobi book store a few days before the safari. In 1953, Brown, a British government officer in Nairobi, set out to unravel the mysteries of the flamingo's behavior, its feeding and breeding habits. His book recounting these findings was published in 1960 by the East African Publishing House.

I nodded my head in agreement when I read Brown's description of the harsh environment in the Rift Valley:

Put your foot down and more often than

Settling in for a nap

not you tread on volcanic rubble; where there is not volcanic rubble there is a fine dust that rises in clouds…Touch a tree and it is thorny; camp near water and you are eaten alive by mosquitos…Sit in the shade and you will sit on a thorn, if not something worse. Such country is not for those who like an easy life.

Well, I certainly wasn't finding life easy! Brown's problem with mosquitoes was of no less concern to me. They would buzz around me by lantern light. The smell of repellent was a fair trade-off for the protection it brought. I also read something that, at the time, I didn't pay much attention to. The words were a prophecy of things to come:

I did not dream that they [the flamingos] would give me the adventures I have had, that I would more nearly come to a sticky end in their pursuit than any other time in my life . . . or that I would behold beauty transcending all my wildest imaginings.

One of the monotonous daily chores was to move the three boxes that held the canoe from one side of the tent to the other. I had to do this to take advantage of the slender band of shade that the tent afforded on each side as the sun crossed the sky. The rubberized boat, which

I was afraid would melt in the heat, was a disappointment. I had hoped to build a blind on it, cast off before dawn, paddle close to the colony, anchor the boat with a stick in the mud, and spend the day photographing the flamingos. But it proved impossible to launch the boat from the broad mud flats that surrounded the lake. Nevertheless, I protected my expensive investment from the sun as I hoped it would be usable on Lake Natron.

Lake Natron was where I had first seen flamingos from the air. Although I was getting great photographs here at Lake Magadi, I felt the need to return to Lake Natron's larger waters. Reading Leslie Brown's book made me wonder if it was possible. He came to the conclusion that due to the immense mud flats and the "crystalline floes, surrounded by dark-red, slimy waters and slush, the Natron colonies of flamingos are as safe from the interference of mortal man as any bird's breeding ground is ever likely to be." I would have to discover the truth of these words for myself.

Customarily, I would read until the late afternoon when the heat became unbearable and remaining active became too difficult. Like the flamingos, I, too, would try to sleep. Many of the great birds slept near the shore, supported by one spindly leg, the other tucked under their bodies. They curved their long necks over their backs, snuggling their heads under a wing. Some birds lazily preened themselves with their tipped beak, carefully fluffing and smoothing feathers. Others drifted on the lake, dipping into the water for a mid-afternoon snack.

Just before sunset, the birds would begin feeding again, and I would go down to the lake for the day's second session of photography. At dusk, the burnt copper tones from the fleeting rays of the sun gave an effect of floating light. The scene was like an Impressionist painting, but with the harsh brush of the Rift Valley.

Returning from the blind, I dined by the light of the propane lantern on the table next to the acacia tree. My mind blank, I would gaze at the stars sparkling in the black sky, listening to the rustling of feathers as the flock of flamingos settled into sleep. To shake me from feelings of loneliness I would play the only music I had brought to camp, a cassette of Arabic music with beautiful undulating rhythm. The exotic sound drifted over the lake, perhaps soothing the gathering of ancient birds as it did me.

Before retiring each night, I cleaned dust from my cameras, prepared film for the next day's work, then folded my two blankets lengthwise to serve as padding against the lava rocks. In the darkness I could hear my furry friend, the tiny mouse, rustle his body in the earth next to a box and settle in for the night.

4

IN THE BUSH

IN THE

Maasai!
At the opening to my tent, shadowed by the late afternoon sun, loomed two tall Maasai warriors, each grasping a steel-pointed spear. They stood there on one leg like the flamingos on the lake—and stared.

Sweat rolled off my arms and legs as I got up, wrapped my *kikoy* around me and stepped toward them. Neither moved. I squeezed past, smelling their bodies: dead charcoal sticks from a campfire. They were well over six feet and each had long hair, plaited and dressed with animal fat and ocher. Their extended earlobes were adorned with beads, buttons, and metal rings. I nodded to them, backing away: their bodies turned, almost imperceptibly, to follow my movements.

Where were Wammasai and Wambugo!

What did these Maasai want? I was on their land, the fiercest part of Maasailand. They could kill me. I remembered hearing about seven German visitors who had journeyed into this part of Maasailand—and were never heard from again.

One of the Maasai nudged me. The cold shock of terror coursed through me, sending frenzied impulses to my brain. *"Why were they here? What did they want? Had I done something stupid; camped in the wrong spot?"*

My mind began to slow. *"Don't be afraid."* Remember, Maasai men, like most African tribesmen, found white women unattractive. "Colorless," an English friend had once told me. "The Maasai think white women are bloody colorless!"

They continued to stare. Well, if this was the poker hand I'd been dealt, I'd better bluff my way through it. Without looking at them again, I began straightening the camp equipment, then edged slowly to the clothesline and lifted off a few pieces of my more delicate laundry. It seemed ludicrous to stand there holding my underwear while two Maasai warriors watched my every

BUSH

move. I continued to stroll about the camp, writing in the film log, dusting off equipment, then, without thinking what I was doing, I grabbed the camera to reload it and accidently fired off a frame.

I looked up and the men were gone. Only the lingering odor of smoke spoke of their presence.

Of course, the camera! Maasai warriors would not allow their pictures to be taken, believing that their spirits would captured on the film.

Wammasai and Wambugo sheepishly trudged down the slope. A lot of help they were! "Tough Mama" had done pretty well without them.

Many times throughout my stay I thought about the two Maasai warriors standing storklike at the entry to my tent—tall, slim, angular young men with chiseled features, curious about the strange woman who had invaded the land they so proudly owned. These were descendants of a

Always the rustling of feathers overhead

people who had walked this valley for centuries.

I wondered what the Maasai thought about the vast colonies of flamingos that inhabited their land with them. I had found very little tribal folklore about the flamingo. Because Maasai are more or less indifferent to anything that does not affect their daily lives, stories of the birds are few. Lions, leopards, hyenas and other predators are prominent in the Maasai tales. Perhaps flamingos are considered merely a part of the scenery, an element in the vast panorama of Africa.

There was one Maasai tale I had read in my research that intrigued me. The Maasai do not believe the flamingo hatches from eggs like other birds. Instead, so the tale relates, the great birds arise from the middle of the lake able to fly at birth, coming up feet first, and assuming a normal upright posture a few feet from the surface. The birds then fly to the edge of the lake to feed. The Maasai believe this birth happens at certain times of the year; at other times, the flamingos descend once more into the lake and hibernate until it is time to rise once again.

This tale is an easy one to explain. Flamingo breeding and egg laying takes place on the mud flats far from shore, and because of the heat waves, the eggs and nests can't be discerned by the Maasai from afar. The mirage effect of pink birds, shimmering above the salmon-hued soda creates the illusion of a flock suspended a few feet above the surface. This vivid reflection makes the birds appear to be upside down in the water, accounting for the Maasai's belief that they come up feet first.

Since flamingos migrate to other lakes periodically and fly during the slightly cooler nights, one can easily see how the tribesman assumed that the flock returns from where they

Receding water levels brought the colonies closer to the shore

came—the hot waters in the center of the lake.

Although the Maasai fascinated and excited me, their sudden and stoic presence in the camp had unnerved me. But I didn't have time to think about possible dangers. I was here to photograph flamingos. And my work was harder than I expected.

Eventually, the hardships and monotony of working in this punishing moonscape of rock began to chip away at my patience. I searched for any excuse to leave camp, but the only one I truly had was to go to the watering hole. I had discovered this shady sanctuary quite by accident. One day, shortly after we arrived, I drove out to look for a different spot from which to photograph the great birds when I saw a tall—perhaps 20 feet tall—acacia tree with green leaves towering above its spindly companions. And below it a patch of green grass. And a pool of water.

An oasis!

I am exaggerating about the pool. This watering hole was nothing more than two fifty-gallon drums that had been cut in half and welded together to form a trough. A single spigot on a long pipe provided a stream of tepid water. I eventually learned that the British, who had built the Magadi soda factory in the 1940s, had extended a water pipe to this remote spot so the Maasai would have fresh water for themselves and their herds of scrawny cattle and goats.

Yet it was an oasis of life in the parched desert. Tiny birds would dart in to take a sip of water from the tank, chirping deliriously at finding such a jewel in the desert. Maasai herdsmen would sit on tufts of grass that had been nurtured by the dripping water and nap or tell stories under the wispy shade of the acacia. Since the time I had been jolted awake by the two warriors at the entry to my tent, I had encountered many other Maasai, mostly elders, herdsmen, women and children and had become at ease in their presence. Every now and then, I would sit next to a Maasai elder in the shadow of the tree, silently sharing the hostile world around us. Two people, from two different worlds, bonded by the experience of living in the Rift Valley.

The watering hole was only a few miles from our camp, but it took an hour driving over the rocky terrain to get there. Occasionally, either Wammasai or Wambugo would accompany me; they also needed a break from the daily routine. We would fill up the plastic water containers which had originally held the fresh water brought from Nairobi and bring them back to camp. Worried about getting sick, I refrained from drinking the water, no matter how desperately I wanted it.

I used some of the water to bathe at camp. Next to my tent I had placed a small square piece of plywood on which I would stand, splash myself with tepid water—there was never a worry about hot or cold water taps—soap my body, then rinse with as little water as possible. The intense heat quickly dried my skin.

Once a week I washed my hair. Why didn't I cut it? In old Hollywood films the heroine whacks off her hair to better endure the rigors of jungle life. I reasoned that anyone who was hardy enough be in such a terrible place, determined enough to defy the heat, the dust, the crawling creatures, and the wild animals, was allowed to keep her hair. It became my test of will, so I kept my hair—if just barely. Tangled strands of it are still hanging like tinsel from the Rift Valley's thorn trees.

One day as I was washing my hair under the spigot, I noticed a beautiful young Maasai girl, perhaps sixteen, watching me. She had a baby in her arms and hugging close to her were two small children and six goats. The goats, half-crazed by the smell of the water, jumped into the tub and splashed around like happy clowns.

Like all Maasai women, the girl's head was shaved, not because of the heat, but as a beauty rite. I'm sure she had never seen blond hair before, and I wondered what she was thinking. I saw her again and again at the watering hole, looking intently at me. I wanted to talk to her, to know her thoughts.

I decided I must try to photograph her or, at least, other Maasai women. About a mile from

One Maasai woman approached me

camp was a Maasai *engang*, a settlement of about twenty mud huts where several families gathered together behind walls of prickly thornbushes which were built to protect themselves and their cattle from lions and other predators. The igloo-shaped huts were made of branches and grass and sealed with a thick layer of cow dung and mud for warmth and dryness during the rainy season. By this time I understood some Maasai habits and knew the men would be out tending cattle or goats while the women stayed behind caring for the children.

I took Wammasai with me, and when I drove up to the the settlement, a group of curious women stood watching me. I smiled, got out of the truck, held out a few coins and my Hasselblad camera and said, "picky, picky," a term which may have sounded childish but one which I had heard Maasai use before.

One older woman looked at the money, then at me, then at the money. She gathered together ten other women, huddled them together and began a spirited, sometimes giggly deliberation. As always, Wammasai looked alert and tense, as if he might suddenly have to run for his life. These women were far more aggressive than the docile women of his tribe.

She proudly displayed all her finery

Suddenly, the women ran to different huts and disappeared inside. Feeling rejected, I got in the Land Rover. I was about to drive away when the women emerged wearing red, blue and yellow beaded necklaces, earrings, and bracelets on their arms, necks and ankles. It must have been all the jewelry that they owned. Unlike the other Maasai I had encountered, these women wanted their pictures taken!

Wammasai held up the photographic reflector while I positioned the women against the dried wall of a hut. My subjects were a little shy at first, but, pleased to have their pictures taken in their finery, were soon smiling into the camera. Because I was a woman—obviously in charge—I had been able to penetrate their anxiety.

We communicated without words

After I finished shooting, I gave each of them some shillings, about two dollars total. As I started to go, the older woman reached out and touched my hand. It was just a light touch, the skin of one hand brushing the skin of another, but it carried with it a warm feeling. Then, each Maasai woman, in silence, lightly touched my hand. A bond had been created and I knew I would never be alone in Maasailand again.

Late one afternoon, restless with the camp, I grabbed my camera and tripod, and with Wammasai, drove across the causeway to the other side of the lake. Gears grinding, we churned up a narrow rutted trail that snaked to the top of the Nguruman Escarpment. We passed a Land Rover rusting in a clump of scrub bushes. Out of a headlight socket popped the head of a curious lizard. Finally we reached the top. Hot dry wind spilled over the edge of the summit so I parked the truck to shield us. From this vantage point the continent of Africa revealed itself. The mag-

The top of the escarpment provided
a new perspective on the flamingos below

nificent Rift Valley split the land. Cradled in its bowl was the blue span of Lake Magadi, and, barely visible, the speck of our green tents on the brown land below. A living chiffon sheet of pink flamingos, dancing to a rhythm that only they could hear, swayed and pulsated over the lake's mirrored blue stage.

Here in this high place I was able to observe the flamingo's behavior from a new perspective, to see things that I couldn't see at ground level. There was a special kind of silence: the wind had ceased to blow. I felt privileged to be standing here viewing one of the greatest sights ever impressed on my visual memory. Even Wammasai, in his inscrutable Kikuyu way, was impressed.

The light was fading rapidly as Wammasai hurriedly unloaded the camera with its huge 900mm lens and, under my direction, secured the tripod's legs in the rubble on the edge of the cliff. I looked through the lens and saw thirty or more flamingos, suspended like living notes on a musical score. It was too beautiful to be real. The camera motor advanced, again and again. Without taking my eye from the viewfinder, I pushed the used film canisters into Wammasai's hand. As I loaded and shot, he steadied the tripod from

the wind that again whipped around the Land Rover. We worked in harmony: hurry before we lose the sun! Then, the color began to melt away, and although there was enough daylight left to shoot more, the magic hour had passed. I relaxed, and backed away from the viewfinder. I knew I had captured the scene.

That is when I saw the two Maasai elders sitting on a rock behind me. Both were old, perhaps eighty and sixty, and the younger one's shaved head was crowned with a swarm of black flies. Their earlobes, stretched long ago by the insertion of wooden ear plugs, were decorated with brightly colored beads. I glanced at Wammasai, but his darting eyes reminded me that he could no more speak with them than I could. There was a stoic patience about the two Maasai and on impulse, I motioned for them to approach the long lens of the camera.

The eldest led the way, leaning for support on a walking stick. Their bony legs were covered in brown dust up to the knees and I thought they must have walked from the nearest Maasai settlement 20 miles away. Still excited, I pointed to the distant flamingos and then to the lens. A glint of apprehension flashed across the older one's eyes, as he moved forward,

One of the greatest sights ever
impressed on my memory

not quite sure what to do. As he bent to the viewfinder, I gently placed my closed fingers over one of his eyes.

"Aaaah!" He jumped back from the camera wildly flapping his thin arms, bellowing a torrent of Maasai words. His startled companion edged to the lens, then leaped back too. They exchanged an incredible babble of words. Neither Maasai had any way of understanding the miracle of 900 millimeters of magnification. To them it must have been as if some mysterious phenomenon had materialized and grown before their eyes.

Strangely, I never thought of taking a photograph of the two Maasai and their animated response to the flamingos. Intuitively, I knew that this was not a picture—this was a real-life experience.

Several days later while driving to the watering hole, I saw a Maasai striding across the dusty land like a prophet of old, planting his spear butt first to guide each step. Hearing the truck, he stood in its path, his solemn eyes demanding a ride. I stopped a few feet from him and he opened the back door and climbed in beside Wambugo.

I had to dodge the Maasai's spear as he compressed his tall frame—he was at least six-and-a-half feet—into the seat. My nose was assailed with the pungent aroma of earth, animals, blood and smoke. He gripped his spear and stared straight ahead as I started out. In the rearview mirror I could see Wambugo's eyes darting like a cheetah's. Wammasai, who was in the passenger seat, eyed me with his "What's this mama doing now?" look. Giving lifts to the Maasai wasn't Wammasai or Wambugo's idea of riding in style.

After a while, the Maasai uttered something to Wambugo who replied with a low drawn out, "Uuuh . . . huummm." The Maasai liked this and spoke again, to which Wambugo replied with a long statement in Swahili. The Maasai must have thought this was amusing because he laughed and began a stream of talk. Wambugo replied with short chuckles and remarks. Soon the two of them were laughing like old drunken friends, yet neither of them understood one word the other said.

Wammasai in the front seat began to snicker, then laugh. I saw the absurdity of the scene as a welcome relief from the heat and found myself chuckling. Soon the four of us were laughing at ourselves and each other. It must have been an odd sight; this white woman, hair flowing in the breeze, giggling with a gaunt Maasai and two Kikuyu tribesmen as we crossed the arid landscape into the fading afternoon light.

As the days passed my initial apprehensions about coping with the elements and the Maasai faded. My tiny camp had become a secure island in the vast sea of the Rift Valley.

It was a comforting fiction that came crashing down upon me one night.

From this high vantage point the desert's beauty unfolded

5

Dance with the Devil

DANCE WITH

There was no shadow on this place except my own. The sun, a white-hot disc radiating jagged fingers of heat, was like an oppressive gravity, transforming simple tasks into tests of endurance. It dragged against my mind causing me to be lethargic and irritable. I could not remember smiling in days. I could feel the hours and minutes of each long day pass through my body like an endless ribbon.

It has been said that it gets so hot in the valley that people go into body shock and can no longer function. I was near that point. I had consciously to force myself to move about: *Get up! Walk to that chair. Now!* The sweat would run from my body: *Move, move! MOVE!*

I'd collapse into the chair, my hand too weary to grasp a pen and write in the daily log. *If the devil lived on Earth,* I thought, *he would surely take up residence at my camp.*

The long shadows that spanned the valley in the late afternoon brought some relief from the sun, and I welcomed the coming night whose approach I had once held in such great fear. The visions of lions ripping through the canvas of my tent disappeared, replaced by empty, exhausted sleep. The tent had become a security blanket, protecting me from all evil, my defense from the *outside.* But one night the fragile walls of my canvas cocoon collapsed around me.

The noise was shattering, a sudden jarring explosion next to my ear. I bolted awake. Panic tore through me like a shaft of ice.

Stampede!

In the blackness just outside the tent hundreds of animals, big animals, battered their way past, a crushing avalanche of crazed beasts. I could smell their sweat and feel the sides of the tent flapping maddeningly as they thundered all around me. At any second the brittle fabric would tear and the animals would smash through. Escape! My thoughts raced for the answer: the acacia outside the tent—impossible; the Land Rover—too far away. Then the

The scorching heat was dulling my sensibilities

THE DEVIL

sinking realization: *there was nowhere to go.* The battering of thousands of hooves rolled on.

"They're going *around* the tent, not through it!" I cried aloud. Then, in a whispered prayer: "They're leaving."

As suddenly as the stampede had come, from nothing to louder than thunder, it diminished and was gone. The concussion of their passing reverberated through me like an aftershock: my sanctuary had been violated.

"Wambugo, Wammasai, Okay?" I called into the night.

After a second came Wambugo's reply, "Okay, *Memsahib.*"

I lay awake thinking how incredibly powerful the stampede had been, how swift and sudden. And how totally defenseless I was in my tent. Should I sleep in the truck? Perhaps bring Wammasai and Wambugo down to my camp? With these thoughts, and feeling vulnerable, I fell back into a fitful, heat-induced sleep.

By sunrise the powdery tracks the animals had left were dusted away by the morning breeze. There was little damage to the camp. The wild animals, whatever they were—zebra, Cape buffalo—must have had radar to miss our tents in the dark. What were they?

Would they return?

Streaks of light filled the dawn sky as I sat in the blind pondering the mystery of the stampeding animals. Across the lake, the heat was already creating undulating, miragelike currents on the horizon. Then I noticed something unusual far in the distance—a disturbance in the mirrored lake. I squinted my eyes. The images began to take shape: shadowy forms of some kind of animal splashing through the shallow water, seemingly walking on its surface. Antelope? They were coming toward my blind, getting closer and closer.

Wildebeests!

Ten or twenty of them; no, forty or more, charging toward me at a full gallop, beating the water into a spray of white soda. I crouched lower in the blind. I could see their long, clown-like faces framed with stringy yellow beards as they charged madly, bucking, kicking, and issuing foghorn grunts. Twenty yards away the wildebeests veered to the side, snorting and splattering mud as they reached dry land and kept running, disappearing at last over a hill in a plume of dust.

Crazy animals! They were like wind-up toys gone berserk. Wildebeests—resembling a horse, a cow, an antelope all in one—looking like cave paintings or leftovers from a prehistoric bestiary. I was perplexed. Why did these cavorting animals come all the way down the escarpment? The water from the soda lakes was undrinkable. And most of all, why had they veered away and

Cavorting
wildebeest
galloped
across the
lake . . .

not crashed in the blind?

This puzzle remained until a few days later when I asked Wammasai to find some wood for the fire. An hour later he had not returned, and I was beginning to feel apprehensive. At last, he trudged into camp hefting an entire ten-foot tree on his back. My instuctions in Swahili had been fragmented, so, not understanding exactly what I wanted, and ever resourceful, he whacked down a whole tree. The tree, which surprisingly had green leaves, was not an acacia and in sign language I asked him where he got it.

Wammasai pointed to the hill over which the wildebeests had disappeared. I set out, plodding up the steep incline until I reached the top. And, there, spread out in the distance, was a marshy area with abundant high grass and dozens of small green trees. Groups of wildebeests rolled in the spring fed waters, snorting and splashing, and prodding their young. I had found the wildebeest's Shangri-La.

What a wonderful campsite this place would make. But my flamingos were not there. I took a lingering look at the green expanse and returned to my dreary camp on the edge of soda-crusted Lake Magadi.

The daily routine of photographing the

flamingos continued, and I began to see predators that lurked near the colony, which I had not noticed before. Although flamingos have been said to be taken by hyenas, jackals, leopards, cheetahs and even lions, the most dangerous raiders are other birds: tawny eagles and marabou storks. It takes a daring, and very hungry, four-footed animal to wander onto the soda flats and try to pad across the glutinous mud, but the eagles, vultures and marabou storks can simply fly over this obstacle.

like the shadow of death

The marabou is a big, evil-looking bird, with a balding skull and a great, greedy beak shaped like huge scissors. The hunched teardrop of its back reminds one of an undertaker on the prowl. Groups of marabou storks walk though flamingo colonies jabbing with their lethal beaks at eggs and week-old flamingos. The hollow cracking of the great bill punching holes through eggs, bone, and skin is a horrible sound. Adult flamingos occasionally raise up and lunge at the larger marabou, forcing it away, but for the most part, flamingos have no defense against this methodical, stalking bird. Sometimes, frustrated by the incessant plundering of their nests, flamingos will form into a solid phalanx and vanquish their tormentors with a coordinated charge.

This defense brings only a temporary reprieve.

The number of flamingos destroyed by predators is high, but it is dwarfed by the numbers that die from natural causes. During my stay, every dawn there was a scattering of flamingo carcasses along the shoreline. These were rapidly disposed of by the "Marabou Litter Patrol" that combed the shore.

Occasionally I would see a flamingo stuck in the hot mud. I hated the helpless feeling of watching a bird, its legs sunk deeply, desperately flapping its wings trying to lift itself skyward. The ooze would cling to its wings, splattering droplets into the air. Finally, exhausted, the great bird would slowly lay down on the black surface, never to escape.

Marabou storks scavenge the shore for fallen flamingos

Yet flamingos have survived since the era of the dinosaur, breeding in their perilous exile, living for up to fifty years.

The flamingo's mating dance is a curious affair, more like a comic spectacle than a display of affection. Leslie Brown referred to it as a "Communal Stomp" as it reminded him of "intoxicated men doing what in Trinidad in my student days we used to call a bram—getting into a huddle to the rhythm of calypso music and making perfect fools of ourselves."

The bill drags up mud for building a nest

This mating dance involves hundreds, perhaps thousands of birds. They pack themselves into a tight mass, breasts pushing against backs, then set off at a fast run as if someone had fired a starter's gun. Then, inexplicably, the birds reverse direction and head back to the starting line. The course is reversed again and again. All of this is accompanied by excited squawks and chirps. Above the mass of bodies rise their necks, a swaying garden of pink, and below a spindly forest of disjointed red legs. It looks like a great centipede whose motor impulses to its thousand legs have gone awry.

This group display by Greater and Lesser Flamingos can be followed by individual dances such as the wing salute where the bird stands stiffly upright, beak pointed to the sky. In this flamingo version of standing at military attention, the bird will suddenly flash open its wings, hold them straight out, then just as suddenly snap them closed. The birds also twist and preen, and stretch a leg stiffly behind them, as if ice skating on the water, until they have attracted a friendly female. The male will follow the female, stretching his neck over her back, touching her with his bill. When the interested female stops, the male mounts her, using his outstretched

A beautiful dance selects the right partner

Even mating is distinctly flamingo

wings for balance.

To lay their eggs the flamingos must find mud with the right consistency for nest-building. The typical nest is a conical mound of mud just over a foot high and the size of a large dinner plate. Across the top the female makes a shallow depression a couple of inches deep for the egg. The nest is built by one of the pair standing astride the nest-site, dipping its beak into the water to the muddy bottom, then dragging the mud between its legs. The mud is then packed into place with the bill and feet. As the nest takes its conical shape, the bird stands on top and continues pulling up mud. The cone is left with a slight hollow in the crown and the egg is laid in this depression. Flamingos normally lay one egg, although the female will lay another after a few days if the first is lost to a predator. I observed flamingos rebuilding abandoned nests left from the previous mating season.

Although the temperature of the brackish slush from which the flamingo drags the mud reaches 140 degrees, the top of the nest, due to the evaporation of water and the coolness of the mud itself, only rises to blood temperature. After the chick hatches and slips from its nest, it must feel as if it is stepping into a hot bath of soda salts.

I had taken many photographs of the flamingos during their mating dances, as well as breeding and nesting, but I wanted to entice the birds closer to the blinds. Why not construct some decoys?

With a ball point pen, I outlined a dozen oval-shaped bodies with squiggly lines on the bottoms of cardboard boxes, then on side pieces drew the necks and heads. Wambugo cut them out with a kitchen knife, carefully following every squiggle. I didn't want to discourage him by saying he didn't have to follow the line perfectly, so I nodded, *"Mzuri sana,"* very good. Wammasai gathered together sticks to use as the flamingo's legs and whittled one end into a sharp point. I took a roll of gray duct tape—a photogra-

I conducted a decoy-making demonstration

Wannasai proudly displays the inventions

waited expectantly. At first the flamingos greeted them with wary indifference, which soon turned to disdain; they weren't associating with a lower and decidedly less animated species. Under the noonday sun, the glue on the duct tape melted, and one by one, the cardboard bodies fell away, leaving only the stick legs standing in the mud.

With more tape, I stuck the decoys together again and set them up on an inlet a short distance from the flamingos. To my satisfaction the birds this time seemed afraid of the decoys and were herded toward my blind.

One day I noticed a frenzy of movement among the flamingos, a ruffling of feathers and nervous squawks. I thought they must be reacting to a predator stalking the colony. Then I

pher *never* travels without duct tape—and tried to fasten on the neck and head. A problem: duct tape won't stick in 120-degree heat. I finally stuck the decoys together in the shade of the Land Rover. I had bought a couple of cans of red and white paint in Nairobi and by mixing the colors ended up with pink decoys. We placed this little flock of cardboard birds on the edge of the lake next to a blind.

On the morning of the decoy's debut we

A blend of paints produced "flamingo pink"

realized—rather *felt*—that the weather had abruptly changed. The temperature suddenly dropped twenty degrees to under 100, giving the air a momentary freshness. A golden haze covered the sun as if a photographic filter had been placed over it. Something odd was happening. I sniffed the air. A rain squall? I looked at Wambugo. He was poised like a startled deer ready to run. *What was happening? Was it rain?*

Whatever it was came down the valley toward us, an ominous hazy, whirling wall of gray and brown carrying desert dust a mile high.

A massive duststorm.

It hit the camp with convulsive fury, darkening the air with swirling dust and debris. Wammasai and Wambugo's tarp was shredded and ripped: the veranda on my tent tore away and snapped wildly on its ropes like a banshee wailing in the wind. Blankets, pots, and tools tumbled toward the lake. The three of us scrambled over the rocks in the choking dust trying to grab anything, papers, laundry, my film log—all of which were being blown toward the lake.

The lashing bits of dust burned into my face and pelted my naked arms and legs as the core of the storm rushed past my ears, whipping my hair across my face and neck. Reaching the

mud flats I retrieved the film log and what papers I could, adding them to the salvaged collection that bulged under my arm.

The flamingos! I thought. Through bleary slits I saw thousands of birds poised motionless in the golden light of the gale, heads curled into their hunched bodies, leaning into the hurling dust and whitecaps. It was a magnificent picture.

I clambered up the slope to my demolished tent, and with my back arched against the wind, loaded the camera. Grabbing a blanket I stumbled blindly down to the shoreline, planted the legs of the tripod in the mud and aimed the long lens at the flamingos. I wrapped a blanket tightly over my head and the camera's body and in that sheltered darkness, oblivious to the stinging wind, shot image after image.

By the time I had fired off the last frame, the wind had calmed. My arms and legs burned as if stung by a thousand insects, and grit clogged every pore of my body, working its way into my nose, my ears, even between my teeth. I was near tears as I looked at the havoc caused by the storm: Wammasai and Wambugo's tent had been ripped apart, and mine was flattened and torn, the rotted canvas unable to withstand the wrath of the wind. Camp equipment was scat-

[handwritten margin note: Whirling dust stung my skin like a thousand bees]

tered like refuse over the rocky terrain. The three of us sat on the rocks, elbows on our knees and faces buried in our hands. We didn't move for a long time.

That night, for the first time, I regretted coming to Africa. Lying on the ground, I cursed the oppressive heat, the terrible land where nothing could survive, the infernal dust, the gritty hardships of this primitive camp. What had happened to my safari, my pleasant excursion into the bush to photograph flamingos?

Where was the safari of my plans—my dreams? The white table cloths, dinner served on china, icy gin-and-tonics in crystal glasses? Where were the bush-wise guides leading me to the mirrored lakes, where I could photograph my flamingos?

I had tried! Even with the shabby equipment and my two untrained workers, I had tried to *stay civilized*. But it was gone. Gone with the heat, the lack of water, the scarcity of food, gone with the rotten safari gear. Gone was the dream. It had become a nightmare.

Powerful winds shredded the tents like paper

(OVERLEAF) The flamingos faced into the golden gale

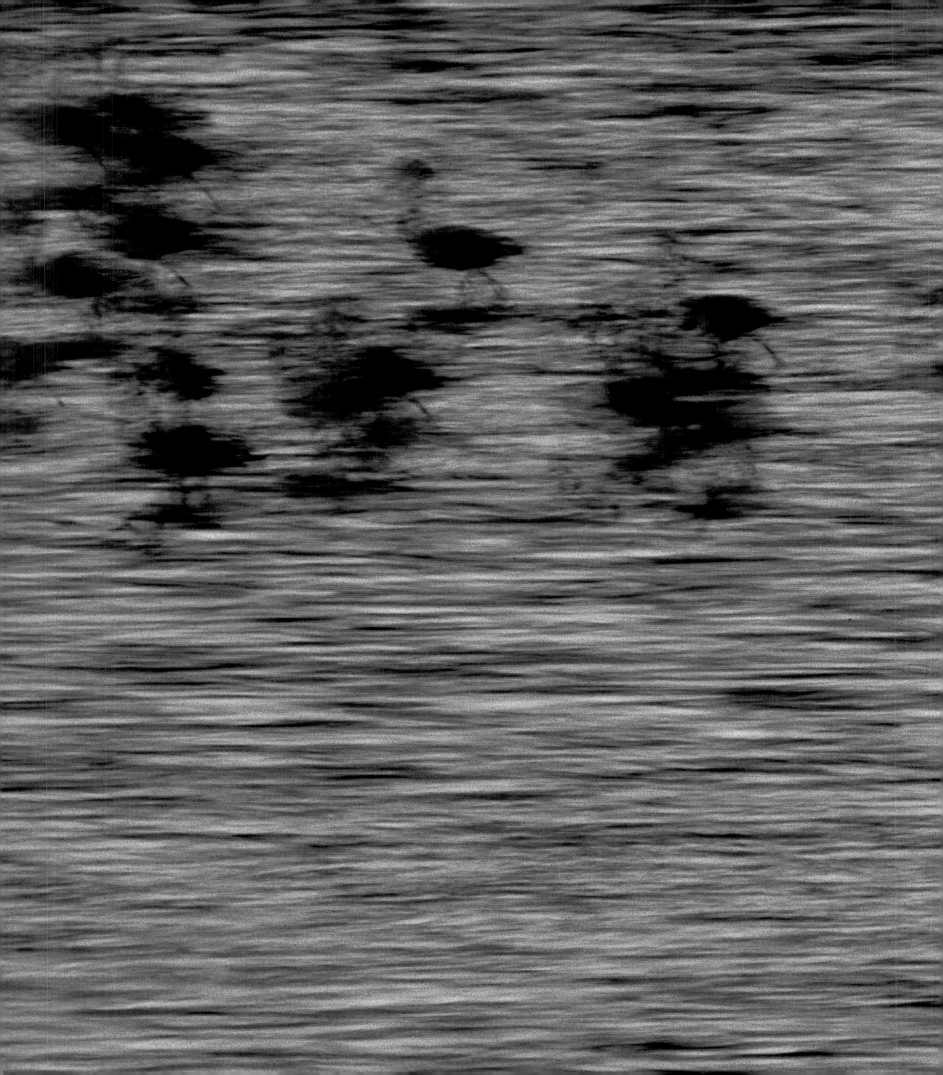

An ominous storm had become a nightmare

SURROUNDED AT SHOMBOLE

SURROUNDED

In the early morning light we repaired the tattered tents as best we could and gathered together the items scattered by storm. I went to the lake and shot several rolls of film, but realized I had documented most of the flamingo's behavior at Magadi. There was only one thing I had to do: go to Lake Natron where I had first flown over the flamingos—and had my first brush with death.

I had to see again the pink island.

Wammasai and I packed the Land Rover for the excursion. Leaving Wambugo to look after the camp, we drove to the causeway and then up the steep path scaling the face of the escarpment. The engine whined as we squeezed past the rusty shell of the truck we had seen several days earlier. At the top, the air was 100 degrees, but refreshing compared to our sweltering camp below. To the south I could see Mt. Shombole which was on the closest edge of Lake Natron. Its volcanic peak, three hours away, was our beacon.

To the west, beyond the rolling hills, spreading in a haze of sand and grass, lay the plains of Serengeti, a vast game reserve that has changed little in thousands of years. I remembered the safari I had taken years before and all the animals I had photographed: lions, their golden coats on fire in the setting sun; elephants, gray visages of an ancient life force; Thompson's gazelles (familiarly called "Tommies"); small, ruddy antelope, walking slowly, cocking heads from side to side as if to shake a burr from the ear.

Heading to Lake Natron, we pushed through tall green grass. Above us, billowing clouds provided relief from the sun, keeping the temperature at a pleasant 90 degrees. I felt as if we were on a Sunday outing. That is until we came upon several Maasai settlements with their mud and dung huts surrounded by a thorny wall of acacia bushes. A young Maasai warrior stared at us intently as we passed. I felt uneasy. We were in a remote part of Maasailand, beyond roads and the rules of civilized society, and it seemed doubtful

AT SHOMBOLE

to me that the man had ever seen a white person before, let alone a white woman.

A glance at the map showed that the village was not marked. We were at the end of the dotted-line road, and ahead I could see the trail diminish into a meager cattle path only half as wide as my truck. Cattle trail or not, I was going to follow it to the end. The dry brush scratched the sides of the Land Rover as we pushed through, dodging holes made by burrowing animals.

A charming warthog came to greet me

A family of warthogs ran across our path: mama, papa, and four little worry warts hoisting the tufts of their tails like flags. The family scurried to an underground burrow where each in turn comically turned around and backed in. Even though the last few days had been a disaster, the antics of these beasts brought a smile to my lips.

The grin vanished when eight Maasai warriors materialized from the bush and stood in a half-circle blocking our path. Their sharp-pointed spears glinted in the equatorial sun. I quickly rolled up the window; Wammasai, in the passenger seat, had his up faster. I turned off the engine, a gas-saving habit I had grown used to.

The crescent of faces stared at us coldly. I smiled weakly and gave a small, tentative wave. The closest Maasai tapped on the window with his spear.

He wants something. I waved. He tapped louder, annoyed, I felt unbearably *aware.* I hated the confrontation, but it was exciting.

I took a deep breath and rolled the window halfway down. The familiar odor of burnt wood curled over the open window. I felt Wammasai stiffen beside me.

The Maasai blurted out a few words. He wanted something. What? I knew they liked Cokes, but I didn't have any with me. Impulsively, I unscrewed the cap from my canteen and pushed the flask out the window. He stared at it. Then, grasping it with slender black fingers, he smelled the opening, raised it to his lips and took a single swallow.

There was no change in his sullen, accusing eyes as he handed the canteen to the man next to him, who swallowed once and passed it on around the circle. The last Maasai finished and held the canteen out to Wammasai who rolled down his window just enough to squeeze it through sideways. Jerkily, he rolled the window up.

I sat there with a pinned-on smile. Then started the engine.

No one moved.

I looked at the camera on the seat next to my hip. It might anger them, but it was worth a try. I slowly lifted the camera, my smile asking if I could take their picture.

Instantly, the eight Maasai warriors scattered into the bush, vanishing as if I had waved a magic wand over their heads. I shrugged at Wammasai as if saying, "All in a day's work." He had a sick look on his face.

Another quarter-mile and the cattle trail quit. We had reached the steep boulder-strewn slope of Mt. Shombole. To our right the Uaso Nyiro river emptied into Lake Natron.

The river was only five feet across, and I could drive across it, if only there were a way to get down to it. A very steep embankment followed the river's edge and blocked any passage. If I tried to push over the edge, the Land Rover would pitch down nose first. The slope of Mt. Shombole seemed equally impassable, the rocks were big as the Land Rover's tires. The truck could tip over. *Damn!* The flamingos were just around that cone-shaped mountain—and I was going to get to them.

I took a gulp of water from the canteen and glared at the boulders on the mountain, wishing that by sheer will power they would disintegrate. *If I couldn't travel over the mountain right side up, I'd climb it sideways.*

I revved the engine and lurched ahead, ascending the mountain at a steep angle. Wammasai

Mt. Shombole
stood
between
me and
Lake
Natron

braced himself stiff-armed against the dash. We were thrown side to side against the doors as the truck jolted over the rocks. My hands clenched the steering wheel in a death grip as it tried to jerk free.

The wheels spun wildly, and there was the smell of burning rubber. I jammed the clutch to the floorboard, pushed the accelerator down and let out the clutch. Rocks rattled down the incline: we started to slide back, then the wheels gripped and the Land Rover leaped forward.

A few more agonizing moments and we had reached a high ridge where we teetered on the edge of an abyss. There was nowhere to go but down. I jammed the steering wheel around as far as it would go and we angled our way down the other side of the slope. Although it looked more harrowing, the ride down was easier. For the first time since we started the climb, I breathed with relief.

There, spread out before us, was Lake Natron. The great expanse of water grasped the sun and bent it back in sharp shafts of light that reflected off our windshield. I could once again see a vibrating pink horizon that appeared to float above the water—the flamingo colony.

I had won!

It was noon. I had a little over an hour, perhaps two, to explore the lake before returning to camp in Magadi. Because of the lack of marked trails, I dared not drive at night. I maneuvered around the base of Shombole, finally parking under the only tree in sight, the ever-present acacia. Before me stretched the white soda flats, a blinding whiteness that, even with the dark sunglasses, made my eyes ache. But, only a quarter of a mile, perhaps a half mile away, was the long quivering line of flamingos. They were very close to the area where I had first seen them from the air. And where my plane almost crashed.

Should I try to walk the soda flats? I remembered too well how close to death Leslie Brown had come trying to cross the flats less than a mile from where I stood. When he started from the shore the chalky flats were, as he said,

Life is a constant struggle against the elements

Many flamingo colonies live protected in the inhospitable center of Lake Natron

"hard and firm enough to land an aircraft on, but soon the surface gave way to pink slushy water." He wrote:

The soda had formed polygonal plates with raised edges rather like giant waterlily leaves. As soon as I could I climbed onto these edges and tried to make my way along them. But they were unreliable and had weak spots and cracked through into the mud beneath, and, as I went on, they grew weaker instead of stronger as they should have done.

Brown floundered on in the terrible heat, always hoping to find sturdier ground. Instead he kept plunging deeper and deeper into the mud, "The effort of wrenching one boot out was often sufficient enough to imbed the other." Realizing he might not have the strength to come back, Brown gave up trying to get to the flamingos. The return over the same terrain was even more hellish: his floundering in the caustic mire caused slivers of soda to become imbedded in his feet. He suffered so terribly from blood poisoning that he nearly lost his legs.

I looked out over the soda flats at the flamingos. They were like a magnet drawing me to them, so, telling myself to be careful, I stepped gingerly on the white surface. The dried soda made a crunching noise, like rock salt underfoot. I took another step. The footing was solid. Another step, then several more. The erratically shaped plates, each about eighteen inches across, gave me the strange sensation that I was walking across a gigantic crossword puzzle, I continued on. The bottoms of my feet soon became hot, burning through the rubber soles of my tennis shoes.

The pink horizon didn't appear to be getting any closer.

A light breeze stirred up puffs of soda, sweeping the fiberglass-like particles into my face. My eyes stung and streams of perspiration trickled in widening rivulets down my skin. The soda was clogging my nose, and I could feel it in

Claret - colored waters

A Clutch of two eggs is rare

If the water level is too low flamingos abandon their nests

my mouth. Breathing became painful.

I felt the ground give a little. Maybe I imagined it. I took another few steps, slowly. No, the plates beneath my feet were shifting. Only a thin crust of soda covered the foul-smelling mud below. If I broke through I'd never get out. I stepped on the next plate and a dark, tar-like goo oozed over the edge of the cracks, spread over the plate—and covered my foot. I felt as if I was watching a clip from a horror movie, but the foot covered in black slime was mine!

That was far enough.

I looked up; the nearest birds *still* appeared to be half a mile away. Lost in a mirage of heat waves, they were two, ten, perhaps twelve miles away. I turned to start the hot trek back and was discouraged to see the shore at least a mile distant. Returning was like walking on thin ice, never knowing if my foot would break through the crusty surface.

Finally, on shore, standing next to Wammasai, who was relieved to see me safe, I took one last look at the flamingos. Now I realized that it was exactly in this spot that Leslie Brown had tried to reach the Natron nesting colony and nearly died in the attempt. Ironically, twenty-five years later—once again in the

Both parents take turns packing mud onto the nest

A diet high in red-pigment helps provide
pink coloration to the feathers

An awkward chick contemplates standing

Security is found beneath the legs of an adult

A juvenile waits two to three years for full coloration

same spot—my plane had almost crashed trying to get closer to the flamingos. And today I had tried again. I had given it a hell of a try, and couldn't get near them. Perhaps no one else would either, at least not on foot.

To Wammasai's surprise I began to laugh. Why? Because the birds were safe. These delicate pink and white flamingo were safe from land predators, both animal and human. They would live and breed in their private sanctuary in the middle of that impenetrable lake—hopefully, forever.

Pretty smart birds after all, I thought.

I started back to the truck when a sudden wave of weakness made me shudder. My skin was cold. Feeling faint, I dropped to my knees, my hands outstretched on the rocks. I tried to rise, but couldn't.

What was happening to me?

Territorial display during nesting is common

(OVERLEAF) A duel of the beaks is never fatal

Ruffled feathers are part of an aggressive defense

7

FLIGHT FROM FANTASY

FLIGHT FROM

"Okay, *Memsahib*."
I opened my eyes to the hot, coffee-scented darkness and heard Wambugo, my camp cook, slide the plastic tray under the flap of the tent. The aroma of the coffee, which had been each morning's lifeblood, now filled me with revulsion. I tried to raise my head from the sweat-soaked blanket, but my body was too heavy. I couldn't move. Squeezing my eyes shut, I retreated into sleep. Slowly the dark cloak of dreams, like the impenetrable African night outside, covered me softly once again.

"*Memsahib?*"

Wammasai's voice this time, from the other side of the canvas. Had an hour passed? A minute? He was somewhere in the darkness with the camera and the heavy tripod, waiting to carry it down to the bird blind at the edge of the lake.

"*Memsahib?*" he repeated, a note of worry in his tone.

"No…no." My mind searched for the Swahili word that would make him leave. "*Memsahib* sick…sick…*mgonjwa*." Go away.

The scraping of his sandals faded across the lava rock. As I drifted back to sleep, I wondered why I couldn't move. *What is wrong with me?*

Suddenly I heard the clatter of pots and pans. The side of the canvas glowed brightly with the morning sun. Wambugo was whistling happily as he prepared breakfast; I could smell the ash-blackened potatoes smoking over the open fire of my camp. Potatoes. The only food I had eaten for more than three weeks.

"Wambugo," I whispered. He stopped for a moment, but the incessant whistling and pot rattling started up again.

"Wambugo," I cried. "Shhh."

"Uh," he answered, still whistling.

"Shhh." I was furious with him. Then I realized he didn't know what "Shhh" meant. Groping for my meager list of Swahili words, I

FANTASY

scanned the crumpled paper, desperately looking for something to make him stop.

"*Memsahib, mgonjwa. Kwenda.*" I am sick, please go. I pushed wet strands of hair away from my face and collapsed on the blanket, wondering how ill I was. I had tried to take care of myself—not drinking the Maasai water, never working in the bird blinds during the furnace heat of the day, eating, eating—what? All the fresh vegetables we had brought had rotted in two days, the tins of meat were gone in a week. Nothing was left but the sickening charred potatoes.

I had consoled myself with the thought that *my body was young enough to take care of itself.* Yet, it had happened. What I dreaded more than anything was sickness. What would happen if I couldn't get up? My tiny camp was perched on the edge of the Rift Valley. No one knew I was here. I was the only one who could drive the Land Rover back to Nairobi. Nor could Wambugo or Wammasai make the long trek over the blistering lava rock on foot.

It was too much to think of. The heat, now reaching 130 degrees, was having a numbing effect on my body—and my mind. Sleep was my escape. I wanted to slip into its dark softness forever.

From outside my tent came a scratching noise on the volcanic rocks, then a strange chorus of cries. What?

I raised myself on one elbow. My hair clung to my face and neck and the cotton *kikoy* covering my body was soaked with perspiration. I breathed heavily: the airless tent was like an oven. The halo of light on the canvas indicated that it was well after mid-day. Had I slept that long?

Images of the drive back from Lake Natron flickered like a silent movie across my mind: the boulder-strewn slope of Mt. Shombole; the scratching of dead acacia trees against the Land Rover; careening down the tortured slope of the escarpment, and finally, the camp, collapsing in my tent. The sickness…

Again the scratching noise, the cries.

What was that sound? With one hand I opened the tent flap. The air, hot but fresh, cleared away the fuzziness. And there, outside, were over a hundred scrawny brown and white goats, their hooves clattering over the rocks, their bleating cries filling the air. A tall, sullen Maasai herdsman stood on one leg watching the goats as they nosed curiously around the camp.

Wambugo was quickly at my side, nodding, worried, a cup of coffee in his hand. "Okay, *Memsahib?*"

I took one sip of the black brew. "Okay, Wambugo," then quickly downed the cup, struggled to my knees and pulled myself into the chair on the veranda. Wambugo rushed off and returned in a moment with another coffee. It helped, my eyes were clearer, but I still ached all over and felt like I had been trampled by a foraging elephant. What I wanted was something to eat—something other than charred potatoes.

A goat brushed against my arm. It smelled horrible, dung and dust. I gasped, my stomach rolling, and pushed it away. No, wait—the goat. Meat! I needed meat for strength. The thoughts tumbled on top of one another: buy a goat; have Wammasai butcher it and Wambugo to cook the meat, or dry it like jerky. Sure, they were farmers, they would know what to do. What about money? Did I have enough Kenyan shillings?

Wambugo handed me another cup of coffee. I put about two dollars worth of shilling notes into his fist, queasily rested the palm of my hand on the head of the goat, and motioned toward the Maasai herder. Wambugo nodded vigorously, then approached the Maasai. Struggling to hide his uneasiness, Wambugo uttered a few guttural words, waved the paper money and pointed to a small white goat.

The Maasai looked disdainfully at the money then said something harsh to Wambugo, who backed away a few steps and looked imploringly at me. Weakly, I waved him back at the Maasai. Wambugo repeated the offer. The herdsman scowled. Wambugo glanced back at me with a "What now?" expression.

This wasn't going to be easy.

I fluttered another ten shilling note in the air, reached for the last two Cokes and with effort put them on the veranda table, then, palms open, indicated they were generously included in the offer.

The Maasai peered at the Cokes, at the money—and at me. He frowned. I pulled out a few more crumpled notes and pushed them into Wambugo's hand. The Maasai glanced at the paper, spit out a few acid words, then crossed his arms and turned his mocking gaze to the horizon.

It was not enough that we had to bargain for a stinking goat, but we were to be insulted as well. Grimly, I slapped a few more shillings into Wambugo's hand—by this time about ten dollars worth, the total of my meager bank account—looked daggers at the Maasai, and turned my back to him. It was all I could do; I wanted desperately to have this haggling end, to go back to sleep.

Wearily, I closed my eyes and thought, *Take it or leave it, fella.*

Silence. Then: "Memsahib?" Wambugo's

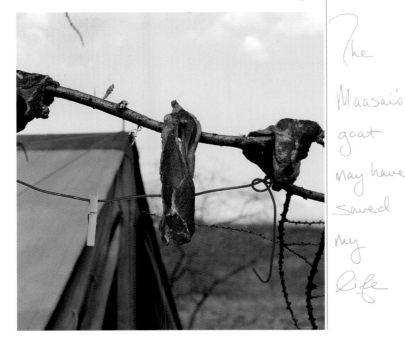

The Maasai's goat may have saved my life

voice was hopeful. I looked around and saw the stoic Maasai nod, almost imperceptibly.

I had haggled–and won.

With Wambugo's help, I stood up, legs unsteady, and walked to where the Maasai was holding out his hand and we laid the money on his cracked palm. The long black fingers and dirty nails closed into a fist, contemptuously crumpling the bills. His shape blurred before my eyes and I almost fell to the ground. It was all I could do to get back to the tent and fall on the blanket.

Several hours later I awoke to see strips of fresh goat meat hanging to dry on the line next to my underclothes. Wambugo rejoiced as he brought over several pieces of half-dried jerky to my tent, letting them hang between his fingers. I looked at the meat closely, it had a suspicious shade of silvery green. *I couldn't eat that!* I motioned to Wambugo to smoke the meat over the fire.

After an hour in the heat and smoke of the fire, the strips were dried dark brown. I watched Wammasai and Wambugo gnaw eagerly on the stringy meat, then I gingerly stuck a piece in my mouth and chewed. And swallowed.

I awoke the next morning, still feeling weak, but alive! After several cups of Wambugo's strong coffee, I got up and walked around. I was okay, still shaky, but okay. Perhaps it was the meat that had helped, perhaps the two nights and a day of sleep. The weeks in the sun had been exhausting, the trip to Lake Natron, the terrible drive over Mt. Shombole, the frightening trek across the soda lake, all had taken its toll on my system. But now my strength was returning.

That afternoon I sat down in the shade of the veranda and went over in my mind what had been accomplished on the safari: how many rolls of film I had taken, what events and beauty I had captured in the photographs, and how much I had learned about the flamingo. It was enough, I thought, closing my eyes. It was more than I had ever imagined. We would leave the next day.

I was awakened from the afternoon's nap by Wammasai's urgent call, *"Memsahib, Memsahib!"*

I placed the patient in a box

Had something awful happened? Outside the tent stood Wambugo and an excited Wammasai. Wammasai gave my arm a little tug and pulled me over to the Land Rover. He opened the back door and proudly waited for me to see what was inside.

I found my self eye-to-eye with a baby flamingo. The bird made a few excited cheeping noises and fluttered awkwardly toward the open door. I blocked the attempted escape with my body then closed the door and turned to face its captor.

Wammasai, chest puffed out, looked like he was ready to be conferred with a medal of honor, awarded for valuable time spent in the field of flamingo research. Either that or this

The juvenile appeared fragile

was his way of saying, "Get well," and "Happy Birthday," all in one. I certainly was not going to dim his shining moment. "Very, very good," I nodded as enthusiastically as I could.

I thought, great, he's caught a baby flamingo, now what are we going to do with it. It couldn't be moved back to Nairobi as it might die. If the bird was slow enough for Wammasai to capture, it may be injured. The wisest course was to hold it for close observation during the rest of the day, and see how healthy it appeared in the morning. Besides it was Wammasai's prize, I couldn't just release it without a little "doctoring".

With a lot of pantomiming, I got my two tribesmen to gather sticks to make a shelter. While they whittled the ends into sharp points, I wove grass into a small mat. With fifty sharp-

A temporary home for overnight observation

ened sticks in hand, we carried them and the mat down to the shoreline and made a four-foot-square enclosure. I chose a nice spot where the flamingo could drink from a fresh water spring, yet have the soda lake for feeding. There was also a mudbar to rest on. Not a bad beachfront condominium, I thought as we pushed the sticks into the ground and laid the grass mat on top for shade.

I held the immature bird's folded wings to its body and carried it in outstretched arms while its legs dangled and its curved neck twisted around to nip at me. It sure acted like it was healthy. At first the young flamingo was bewildered in his strange home, but was soon dipping its beak into the lake, eating and drinking.

Wammasai built a pen on a mud bar

The next morning at first light the three of us looked into the pen and were rewarded by happy chirps and squawks. The flamingo didn't peck at me as I lifted it out of the pen and set it in the shallow water. It stood there for a moment, then realizing the barrier was gone, cheeped loudly, and ran across the surface of the water with its webbed feet, wings flapping—to home.

We walked back to the camp and Wammasai and Wambugo collapsed the tent and packed it on the Land Rover while I busied myself getting the boxes of film together. As I lifted the last box, the tiny mouse I had shared my tent with for the past month, darted for the cover of a nearby lava rock. Each night when I had heard him nibbling close to my ear, I felt comfortable. I was not quite so alone.

The mouse scurried from the meager shade of the burning rock to another, rested briefly, panted rapidly, then scampered off to find other shelter from the fierce heat. Sadly, the shade and comfort of my tent had been taken from him. There was no place for him to feel cool and protected. I watched as the desperate little creature sprinted away across the dust.

"Goodbye," I said softly, and walked quickly to the waiting Land Rover.

Behind me I heard the familiar rustling of feathers as thousands of flamingos took flight.

I didn't look back.

I glanced down into the

spreading rings of water

and saw my own reflection

After a month in Africa

I realized my quest had ended

APPENDIX

FLAMINGO — *Latin for flame*

In the animal kingdom, flamingos are classed in the order *Ciconiiformes*, which includes pelicans, storks, herons, bitterns and some other shore birds; their family classification is *Phoenicopteridae*.

Phoenicopterus, the family designation for most of the flamingos in this book, is derived from Greek and means crimson-winged. The species designation *ruber* (assigned to the Greater Flamingo) means red or bright red, and the subspecies designation *roseus* (also assigned to the Greater) means red or pink.

Six different kinds of flamingos have been identified. There is some disagreement, however, whether all six should be regarded as separate species or whether some should be subspecies.

GREATER FLAMINGO *Phoenicopterus ruber roseus antiquorum*

The Greater Flamingo is much paler compared to the other kinds of flamingos with body and head and neck white tinged with pink. The brightest crimson color is on the back edge of the wing. The bill is black on the outer half and the rest is pale pink extending back into the face around a yellow eye. The legs are bright pink.

The Greater male stands five feet tall, usually larger than the female. Males weigh between seven and nine pounds, females average two pounds less. The Greater Flamingo has the widest territorial distribution of all the flamingos. It lives throughout the Mediterranean and Africa and often migrates between these areas.

LESSER FLAMINGO *Phoeniconaias minor*

The family designation *Phoeniconaias* translates as "crimson water-nymph." *Minor* is self-explanatory.

The Lesser Flamingo is the smallest of the flamingos. There is little difference between the sexes. When standing, the male is just over three feet tall, the female slightly smaller. The head and neck of the adult Lesser is a darker pink than that of the Greater. The back and wings are a deep crimson. The bill is dark red, extending back from the eye, appearing almost black. The legs are bright red. The Lesser lives almost exclusively in Africa, concentrating in the Rift Valley. However, some groups of this flamingo have been noted in India and the southern Red Sea. The Lesser is the most numerous of the flamingo species.

CARIBBEAN FLAMINGO *Phoenicopterus ruber ruber*

The Caribbean, or as it is sometimes referred, the American Flamingo, is the most colorful of the six flamingos as the *ruber ruber* name indicates. The plumage of the Caribbean is almost totally red, with deep orange-red accents. The adult male and female appear identical, although the male is up to twenty percent larger. The male stands about five feet tall and has a wingspan about the same size. Males weight between seven and nine pounds, the females two pounds less. The Caribbean Flamingo is confined to the Caribbean Islands with an outpost on the Galapagos Islands in the Pacific.

ANDEAN FLAMINGO *Phoenicoparrus andinus*

The Andean Flamingo is also similar in size to the Greater. It often gives the impression of being stouter, although this may be due to its thick plumage.

The adult's head, neck, and upper breast are tinged wine red, a distinguishing mark. The bill is yellow at the base, the outer half black. There is a red spot between the two nostrils on the upper mandible. The iris is orange-brown. The feet and legs are uniquely yellow. The Andean Flamingo lives mostly in a small area in the Andean high plains, but is also found in southern Peru, northern Chile, and parts of Bolivia and Argentina.

CHILEAN FLAMINGO *Phoenicopterus chilensis* (sometimes *Ph. ruber chilensis*)

The Chilean Flamingo is sometimes treated as a subspecies of the Caribbean Flamingo. It has much similarity to the Greater Flamingo in size and coloring although it is slightly smaller. The adult Chilean is a very pale pink fading to white on the head. Long crimson feathers color its back and tail. The bill is black turning to pale pink. The legs are a gray with bright pink feet and "knees". The Chilean is the most numerous of the South American flamingos, finding a home in most areas of the continent.

JAMES' FLAMINGO *Phoenicoparrus jamesi*

Smaller than its three South American cousins, the James' Flamingo is only slightly larger than the Lesser Flamingo of Africa. It has white-toned plumage delicately layered with pink and carmine spots on the breast. The legs and feet are orange-red. The bill is a carnival of color: orange-yellow, and black, with a carmine band that extends back to the eye. The James' Flamingo prefers to have its home in the salt flats of the high plains of the Andes, but some live in the extreme south of Peru as well as in Bolivia, Chile, and Argentina.

SELECTED BIBLIOGRAPHY

Beard, Peter. *The End of the Game*. San Francisco: Chronicle Books, 1988.

Brown, Leslie. *The Mystery of the Flamingos*. Nairobi: East African Publishing House, 1973.

Isak Dinesen (Karen Blixen). *Out of Africa*. New York: Vintage Books, 1985.

Markham, Beryl. *West With the Night*. Berkeley: North Point Press, 1983.

Ogilvie, Malcom & Carol. *Flamingos*. Gloucester: Alan Sutton Publishing Limited, 1986.

Saitoti, Tepilit Ole & Beckwith, Carol. *Maasai*. New York: Harry N. Abrams, Inc., 1988.

ACKNOWLEDGEMENTS

My deep gratitude goes to Dr. Allan Johnson at the Institute of Biology Nature Reserve in Camargue, France for his kind reading of my manuscript and permission to reproduce the photograph on pages 82–83. Thanks also goes to Jorg Hess and Adelheid Studer, whose research in the field of flamingo behavior was generously shared with me as an aid in completing my own work.

I will always be indebted to my special friend Roberta Montgomery Fonville, who taught me much about being a woman in Africa. I am especially grateful to Cork Millner for his editorial contribution and to Tom Lewis for sensitivity in graphic design.

Particular thanks are also due to other people who helped me along the way: Donna Humberd, Ivan Kronja, Richard Breitung, George Tamas, Kurt Borer, Linda Hardcastle, Bill Downey, Shayla Waite, Don Humberd, James Beckett, Steve Rahm, Armando Flores, Christine Liotta and Sindie Sardo.

And a very special thanks to Robert Morton at Abrams, whose ongoing support helped make this book possible.